365

**TEN-Minute
Solutions to**

MAKE YOUR
HOME HOMIER

365 TEN-Minute Solutions to

MAKE YOUR HOME HOMIER

Beautify the Interior
of Your House

Fair Winds Press, Inc., a member of
Quayside Publishing Group
100 Cummings Center
Suite 406-L
Beverly, MA 01915
(978) 282-9590
www.fairwindspress.com

10 09 08 07 06   1 2 3 4 5

Editor: Barbara C. Bourassa
Cover design by Doublemranch.com
Book design by Sheila Hart Design, Inc.

Printed and bound in Canada

Table of Contents

Chapter One:
SPRING

Step inside and inhale.

If you're at home a lot, you might get so used to pet, mildew, or even cooking smells that you don't notice them anymore. Every few months, take a walk outside for a few minutes and then come back in your front door and breathe deeply (or have an objective party do it for you). Then tackle the smells as needed—opening windows, turning on fans, taking out the garbage, cleaning the debris trap in the sink, setting out small bowls of vinegar to absorb musty air, spraying a very lightly scented (linen, fresh laundry) antibacterial spray in the bathroom, or lighting a few lightly scented vanilla or cinnamon candles to get rid of the odors you don't notice anymore.

Put a plush area rug in your entry area.

Thick, soft materials emphasize the earth element and provide a sense of security, comfort, and stability. A plush area rug in your foyer or front hall gives everyone who enters your home a warm welcome.

Accent your staircase.

Paint the risers on your stairs an accent color to add interest.

Paint your entry area yellow to promote good cheer.

A foyer or entry area seems cheery and bright when it's painted sunny yellow. A yellow entrance makes visitors feel welcome, especially in the winter or in a foyer that lacks natural sunlight.

Weatherstrip exterior doors.

Worn or missing weatherstripping costs you money every day.
Self-adhesive products are easy to use, but it's really worth the
effort to install metal weatherstripping. Measure the height
and width of the door and cut metal V-channel to fit. Tack
the strips to the doorjamb and the header, inside the stops.
To keep the channel from buckling, work from the top down.
When the strips are in place, use a putty knife to pull them
into position, between the door and the jambs, when the door
is closed.

Pay attention to what's reflected in a mirror.

Because mirrors reflect whatever is before them, they double the energies of objects. When you hang a mirror in your hallway, pay attention to what it reflects. In front of a mirror, position decorative items that represent qualities you desire and let the mirror "double" their benefits.

Pick two tones for your doors.

You can easily accentuate doors by painting the frames one color and the door itself another color.

Hang a landscape with a distant view on an obstructing wall.

Here's a technique for symbolically expanding a confined space: Hang a picture of a landscape with a faraway view on the obstructing wall. This image creates an illusion of openness and distance.

Dust the television with a sheet of fabric softener.

The static guard will keep dust from resettling. If anyone in the house is sensitive to perfumes, make sure to buy sheets without scent.

To keep mini-blinds clean, dust them weekly with a lamb's wool duster.

Make sure to close the blinds first, and remember that both sides get dirty and require dusting. A lamb's-wool duster is also good for lampshades because it attracts dirt and won't leave a residue the way a rag might.

Display a peacock for respect and good fortune.

In China, peacocks are viewed as symbols of respect, beauty, and good fortune. Display an image of a peacock in your living room to attract these qualities.

Place six candles on the mantelpiece.

In many homes, a fireplace or woodstove is a source of comfort and relaxation, where people sit together to socialize. By placing six candles on your mantel, you encourage positive exchanges with friends and loved ones. Symbolically, this number also invites household members to share their possessions, experiences, abilities, and affection with one another.

Burn lavender-scented candles in your living room.

To encourage peaceful feelings or relaxation among friends or family members, burn candles scented with lavender or vanilla essential oils. (Note: Synthetic fragrances don't produce the same effects as pure essential oils.)

Dust your books.

Wipe lightly with an untreated, soft flannel or microfiber cloth to dust books. Dusting spray or polish tends to just smear the dust around, as does pressing too firmly.

Place an aquarium in your living room for good luck.

According to the principles of feng shui, all living things are considered lucky. Aquariums—especially when filled with goldfish—are thought to be particularly fortunate. (Notice how many Chinese restaurants feature aquariums in their décor.) To improve relationships with friends and family members, place a fish tank in your living room.

Use pink, peach, or yellow in the living room.

Colors affect us psychologically, even if we aren't aware of it. Pink, peach, and yellow inspire sociability, optimism, and feelings of affection. Consequently, they are good colors to include in living and family rooms. Yellow can promote upbeat feelings and good cheer, especially in a room that doesn't get much natural light, or in a cool, north-facing area.

Eliminate cat urine odors with orange.

An off-the-shelf orange cleaner, like 409 Orange Power, works better than the products that are specially designed to deodorize cat urine. It costs about half as much, but it covers the odor well enough that other cats aren't drawn to the same spot to do their worst.

Give books breathing room.

Even though it seems like it's saving space, don't double-shelve books. To keep books from mildewing and molding, provide air circulation above and behind them. This means just one row of books per shelf, and an inch or so between the top of the books and the underside of the shelf above. This approach makes it easier to dust the books and shelves, too.

Choose a round table to facilitate congeniality and unity.

Because circles symbolize unity and cooperation, eating together at a round dining table can help increase congeniality among household members. Think of the term "roundtable discussion," which suggests give-and-take. Unlike a rectangular table, which has a head and a foot, a round table doesn't contain hierarchical symbolism.

Consider installing French doors to divide rooms.

With French doors, you can create a separation between rooms without the permanence of a wall. When you want to conserve heat or air conditioning, provide privacy, etc., you can shut the doors. Because you can still see through the glass panels, however, a sense of spaciousness remains. Hint: Doors with grilles look better in older homes.

Buff wooden floors to a soft glow.

Once or twice a year, apply a coat of clear bowling alley paste wax to a wood floor, then buff it with a commercial buffing machine (available at tool rental stores). The wax will restore the floor's luster and help conceal scuffs.

Place a rectangular area rug under your table.

A rectangular rug in your dining room will spur growth.
If you'd like to increase your family's size or expand your social
circle, use a rectangular rug—especially one that includes
green or blue in its design—under your table.

Hang drapery to divide rooms.

Give your home an Old World look by hanging handsome drapery—velvet or tapestry, for instance—between two rooms as a divider. This pretty treatment also has a practical side. Drapery can prevent drafts and keep heat contained in a particular area when hung between a living room and a hall or stairway. When it's not in use, tie back the drape with a pretty tasseled cord.

Position two chairs at the table for romance.

The number two symbolizes partnership, so if your goal is to inspire romance, place two chairs at your dining table. To encourage closeness and cooperation in a relationship, put one chair at the head of the table and one at the side, rather than at the head and foot, which places a symbolic barrier between the two individuals.

Consider adding wainscoting to the dining room.

Durable wood wainscoting protects walls in areas that get a lot of use, and it gives any room a classic, homey feel.

Install picture rail molding.

Here's an attractive way to display your favorite works of art. Instead of simply hanging pictures on nails hammered into the walls, attach decorative molding at the top of a wall or walls. Put picture hooks into the moldings and suspend paintings from wires or cords hung on the hooks. Hint: Use 50-pound clear fishing line for hanging artwork from a picture rail molding. It's practically invisible.

Use red place mats for good luck.

To double your possibilities for good fortune, especially in money matters, use red place mats underneath your dishes.

Combine warm and cool colors to create balance.

A combination of warm and cool colors in your dining room can produce harmonious feelings among diners. Choose complementary hues for best results: Use pink or red with green; peach or orange with blue; or yellow with purple.

Arrange your artwork before you hang it.

Before you start pounding nails into the wall, lay out your artwork on the floor. Move pictures around until you arrive at a configuration that you like. This way, you're sure to be happy with the final result.

Skip the dish rack.

Do away with that bulky dish-draining rack if you hand-wash dishes infrequently. Instead, use a clean bath towel on the rare occasions when you need to air-dry dishes.

Hang a mirror above the stove.

According to the Chinese principles of feng shui, the stove is considered a source of good luck and prosperity. Because mirrors visually "double" the power of whatever objects they reflect, hanging one above your stove symbolically doubles its power to bring you good fortune. A mirror serves another purpose here, too. When the cook is preparing food, he may not be able to see people entering the kitchen—the mirror allows the cook to see behind him without turning around.

Avoid cabinets with glass doors.

Cabinets with glass doors are great if you have lots of pretty dishes or stemware to display, but unless you're exceptionally neat they aren't a practical choice for most kitchens. Glass doors reveal clutter and show fingerprints.

Keep your stove clean and in good working order.

A stove can only generate good luck if it is functioning properly. A damaged or dirty stove will produce the opposite effect. In feng shui, the stove is also connected with health—here is where the cook prepares food to nourish the household members. Make sure your stove is clean and in optimal condition, so you can attract health and wealth into your home.

Consider adding roll-out trays to provide easy access.

If you add full-extension, roll-out trays to base cabinets, you'll never have to get down on your hands and knees and rummage around to reach something in the back. This is ideal for storing pots, pans, large casserole dishes, and other heavy items, as these convenient trays also let you get organized and reduce cabinet clutter.

Leave space beside the fridge for groceries.

Position a cabinet or work surface beside your refrigerator so you'll have a convenient place to plunk bags of groceries.

Choose granite countertops for elegance.

Granite countertops add a touch of luxury to a kitchen. According to experts in the field, granite countertops are one of the most popular home improvements today. Beautiful and durable, they come in a wide range of colors and patterns.

Use green in your decorating scheme to promote good health.

From both a symbolic and a practical perspective, feng shui links the kitchen with health. Green is the color of vegetables and plants, so this color has positive associations with nutrition. When you include green in your kitchen's color scheme you demonstrate your desire for good health and invite well-being into your home.

Install a ceiling fan.

A ceiling fan can help reduce both heating and cooling costs by circulating the air in your living space. From the perspective of feng shui, ceiling fans placed in public areas of your home also help to keep your social life from languishing.

Use your stove every day.

If you don't use your stove regularly, you'll limit your good fortune. Turn on the stove and boil water every day, even if you don't actually cook anything.

Steer clear of hollow-core interior doors.

Hollow-core interior doors, usually made of mahogany veneer panels, are an inexpensive option, and they look it. Not only are they totally without character, sound travels right through them, and the thin wooden veneer chips easily and can be broken through without much effort. Opt for solid wooden doors inside your home for durability as well as aesthetics.

Vary your lighting sources.

Use different types of lighting in your kitchen and/or living areas, both for convenience and aesthetics. A combination of ambient, task, and mood lighting is best.

Design a wall mural between countertops and wall cabinets.

Colorful ceramic tile combines beauty with durability when mounted on the walls between countertops and the bottoms of your wall cabinets. Inexpensive and easy to clean, decorative wall tile lets you be creative. Combine plain and patterned tiles, intersperse different shapes and colors, even design a mural. Graph your design to scale on paper before you start adhering tile to the walls.

Add visual texture with granite chips.

Does your kitchen have old plastic laminate on the walls between the countertops and upper cabinets? Cover it up with wall covering made from granite chips to add visual appeal and texture.

Consider the contents of your water.

Minerals or chemicals in your water supply may adversely affect some materials. Water that contains a lot of iron, for example, can leave rust stains on light-colored porcelain. Make sure the sinks and faucets you select are made of materials that won't be damaged by your water.

Choose a ceramic tile floor to promote security.

According to the Chinese element system, ceramic tile falls into the earth category, which is linked to feelings of security and comfort. Choosing a ceramic tile floor for your kitchen can help promote these qualities in your domestic life. It can also help secure your financial assets.

Hang a plant above your sink to prevent financial losses.

According to the principles of feng shui, the drains in your home literally drain energy from your environment. To keep money from going "down the drain," hang a plant above your sink. Plants, which symbolize life and growth, serve to offset the devitalizing quality of the drain. Plants with red or purple flowers are best.

Baking soda is a bathroom basic.

You can use baking soda to clean all the surfaces in your
bathroom except the window and the mirror. Use it in place
of chemical scouring powder to get grime out of the tub or
sink. For chrome and tougher spots, make a paste from baking
soda and work with that. Baking soda's also handy for cleaning
bathroom tiles. Just sprinkle some on, scrub it off with a damp
cloth, and wipe clean with a damp mop or sponge.

Consider adding a soaking tub.

Hippocrates believed "the path to health is a scented bath and a daily massage." To indulge yourself with regular, long soaks in a hot bath, you may want to install an extra large soaking tub in your bathroom. Choose from lots of styles and options. High-backed slipper tubs, old-fashioned claw-foot tubs, free-standing pedestal tubs, extra-deep Japanese soaking tubs, and whirlpool and spa models. Transform an ordinary bathroom into a personal retreat.

Hang a plant in the corner above your bathtub.

The mist from your shower or bath will nourish the plant and keeps it healthy.

Kill mold or mildew on tile or grout with chlorine bleach.

Mix one part bleach and two parts water in a labeled spray bottle you reserve just for this purpose. The surface should be dry before you start, and test a small, hidden spot first to make sure you're not going to harm the finish. Then spray the mold or mildew with the bleach concoction, let it sink in for 10 to 15 minutes, scrub it with a brush, and rinse thoroughly. Don't breathe in the bleach, and keep the area well-ventilated while you work and for several hours after. If you are uncomfortable using bleach, try a commercial oxygenated cleaner.

Separate the tub and shower.

If you're designing a master suite, choose a separate tub and shower stall arrangement instead of the ordinary all-in-one combination. This attractive and versatile plan allows you to customize your bathroom to suit your individual cleansing style. Build a roomy, walk-in shower area with lots of options—body spray jets, hand-held shower, steam only, even a personal rainforest! A deep soaking tub, with or without whirlpool jets, provides soothing luxury.

Place a vase of fresh flowers near the bathroom sink.

According to the Chinese principles of feng shui, this will help keep positive energy from draining away. Fresh flowers add a pretty accent in your bathroom, too. Red or orange flowers are best—the fiery colors offset the preponderance of water in a bathroom.

Spotlight the sink.

The convention used to be to match the sink, toilet, and tub. However, it's more fun to choose a sink in a different color or material as an accent. Consider a brightly patterned porcelain sink, perhaps one painted to resemble Mexican pottery or blue-and-white Delft china. Hammered copper or pewter sinks add a handsome touch in a traditional bathroom; colored glass sinks put pizzazz in a contemporary setting.

Use red or orange in your bathroom's color scheme.

To offset the strong water element that naturally predominate in a bathroom, choose vibrant fire colors—red or orange—to create balance. Towels, shower curtains, bath mats, and other accessories will do the trick. If you aren't comfortable with such bright colors, choose a softer tone, such as rose, peach, or even sunny yellow.

Give an old washstand a new role.

Consider updating an antique washstand by turning it into a bathroom vanity. Hint: Choose an old-fashioned milk-white porcelain sink or one that's painted with little flowers to mimic the wash basins and pitchers that sat on washstands before the days of indoor plumbing.

Put a bench in your bathroom.

Provide a place in the bathroom to sit comfortably and put on your shoes, clip toenails, or perform other routine personal hygiene tasks. Benches designed for exterior use are ideal in a bathroom, because they can withstand wet conditions. An outdoor bench made of teak, cedar, wrought iron, or wicker makes an attractive and practical addition to a bath or dressing area.

Let there be light.

Consider installing a skylight above your shower to let the sun shine down on you while you wash. It's the next best thing to standing under a waterfall.

Change your vanity pulls.

Give your bathroom a quick pick me up by changing the pulls on the vanity. Choose something colorful, whimsical, or dramatic—have fun.

Protect a marble vanity top.

Marble, with its extensive range of colors and patterns, is a lovely choice for a bathroom vanity top. But this porous material must be protected from water and other liquids to keep it looking its best. Seal it with stone or patio sealer (available in most hardware stores).

Vacuum like a clock.

Both to make sure you don't skip part of the floor and to make the most of your time, start vacuuming to the left of the bedroom door and proceed around the room in a clockwise fashion until you reach the door once more, so you can take the vacuum out with you.

Choose a pretty color for your bedroom ceiling.

Who says ceilings have to be white? It's more interesting to let a ceiling echo one of the colors in your furnishings—especially in the bedroom, where the ceiling is often the first thing you see when you wake up.

Paint a guest room green to inspire serenity.

Green is a color that encourages restful feelings. Paint the walls of your guest room green to suggest the serenity of a peaceful forest or meadow.

Add a small fridge to your master suite.

Do you enjoy a glass of milk before bed or wake up hungry during the night? Put a small refrigerator in the master suite to keep drinks and snacks handy. Fit it into your closet or install it under your bathroom counter for convenience.

Include thick, plush fabrics to provide a sense of security and well-being.

Thick, soft, heavily textured fabrics—particularly those made of natural fibers—bring the earth element into a bedroom. Because the earth element enhances security and permanence, using plush rugs or nubby-textured bedspreads can be comforting to young children and adults alike.

Store stuffed animals in a basket in the corner.

Even when your child outgrows her stuffed animals, it's nice to keep them around to remind her of the people who so kindly gave them to her.

Mist your guest room with a calming scent.

To help guests relax and feel comfortable in your home, mist their room with a soothing scent, such as vanilla or lavender.

Store books in a big basket.

Place a book basket in every room so that your guest or child can choose one to read any time is strikes them.

Paint a guest room blue to encourage restful sleep.

Blue's soothing qualities help relieve stress at the end of the day and promote rest and relaxation. Paint the walls of your guest room blue to help guests sleep soundly, or decorate the bed with blue sheets and linens.

Organize children's hair accessories in a caddy.

Do you have a little girl? If you do, then you know how many hair accessories one girl can accumulate! Instead of throwing hair accessories into a dusty bathroom drawer, organize them in a plastic caddy with dividers for separating barrettes, elastics, hair bands, and clips. Little girls love to pick out their own outfits at a very early age, and this way they can see all of their hair accessories and quickly choose one before heading off to school.

Use a brown or tan rug to steady emotions and increase trust.

Brown, an earth color in both Eastern and Western traditions, can help a nervous or very sensitive child feel more safe and secure. Because a rug symbolizes one's footing, place a brown or tan rug in the child's bedroom to provide a stable foundation.

Hang purses and backpacks on a coat hook.

The doorknob can hold only so much! Depending on how many backpacks and purses your children have, you might want to consider mounting a coat hook to hold them. That way they are off the floor and out of the way.

Paint a guest room peach to attract happiness.

Peach blends the optimism of yellow with the affection and congeniality of pink. Paint your guest room peach to create a pleasing, cheerful mood for visitors.

Decorate with metal furnishings to encourage structure and determination.

In the Chinese elemental system, metal is associated with strength, permanence, stability, and focus. Metal furniture, such as a brass bed or a metal desk, can improve a person's persistence and concentration. The metal element also provides a sense of stability and structure for children whose lives are in flux or who feel insecure. To prevent stasis, however, consider combining metal furnishings with some wooden pieces (which stimulate expansion).

Put all costume jewelry in a box with compartments.

If you don't store jewelry properly, everything gets tangled and it's impossible to sort out. Avoid this disaster by choosing a jewelry box with separate compartments for earrings, necklaces, rings, and bracelets.

Decorate with wood furnishings to encourage growth.

In the Chinese elemental system, wood is associated with expansion. Wood furniture helps stimulate healthy growth, mentally, physically, and emotionally. To modulate growth, however, combine wood furniture with metal pieces.

Affix reading lights to the headboard wall.

Instead of placing lamps on the nightstands, install reading lights on the wall on either side of the bed. Hint: Fixtures with adjustable rods and dimmer switches allow versatility.

Select big, monotone pieces for a small room.

Filling a small room with dinky furnishings gives the impression of being in a dollhouse. Instead, select a few attractive pieces of furniture and let them make a bold statement. Eliminate clutter, stick with solid colors instead of patterns, and reduce accessories to a minimum to keep the space from seeming cramped.

Hang two bells on a doorknob.

Tie two bells on the doorknob of your master bedroom to encourage romantic harmony.

Install a hook on the back of the door to hang hats and caps.

Sunhats, baseball caps, spring bonnets, winter hats, and fun character hats crowd lots of kids' closets. To organize them, install one or more hooks on the back of the bedroom door. If you hang the hooks at your child's eye-level, they'll be able to pick and choose themselves.

Use vanilla incense to produce feelings of comfort and contentment.

Vanilla is a calming scent and can help ease stress and anxiety. It also reminds many people of baking and sparks other nourishing memories. Burn vanilla-scented incense in a child's room to instill feelings of comfort and contentment.

Consider moving your washer and dryer to the bed/bath suite.

Most laundry is generated in the bedrooms and baths, so it makes sense to put the washer and dryer here, rather than in a kitchen or basement.

Take heavy comforters or blankets to the laundromat.

Washing heavy bedding in your home machine can mean a costly and inconvenient broken washer at worst and improperly cleaned covers (the soap and water don't reach into the folds) at best. Instead, invest your 10 minutes in driving time and take those heavy covers to a laundromat.

Convert a closet into a mini-office.

A closet can quickly become a small, handy office. If the closet's interior is wide enough, place a pair of two-drawer file cabinets left and right, then lay a piece of wood, stone, glass, or plastic on top to form a double-pedestal desk.

Use metal furnishings to promote stability.

According to the Chinese principles of feng shui, the metal element increases strength and permanence. If your goal is to improve stability or structure in your company's business or finances, choose metal furnishings for your office.

Control power cord clutter.

Rein in your electrical cords by housing them in plastic channels that can be mounted to your baseboards.

Choose a gray carpet to improve security.

Gray is a "metal" color and can enhance stability in your
business. By placing a gray carpet underfoot, you symbolically
establish a sound foundation in your workplace and improve
your own (or your employees') sense of security.

Label electrical cords.

Don't guess which electrical cord is which. Label them with
small, individual tags that identify what connects to what.

Use yellow in your decorating scheme to encourage optimism and creative thinking.

Sunny yellow helps us feel more cheerful and positive. To boost your spirits and stimulate creative thinking, paint your office walls yellow.

Have ungrounded outlets replaced.

Ungrounded electrical outlets can cause power glitches that may adversely affect your computer and other equipment. Have them replaced with safer, properly grounded outlets.

Use lateral file cabinets instead of vertical ones.

Lateral files provide more usable storage than vertical ones. They're more convenient, too. Hanging file folders don't get lost in the back of drawers, and because the drawers aren't as deep, they don't stick out so far into the room when open. You can use the top of a lateral file cabinet as an extra work surface, too.

Paint your office door red.

Share good luck with everyone who enters your office by painting the door red, the Chinese color of luck. Each time you go in or out, you'll remind your subconscious to bring good luck your way.

Consider adding built-in bookcases around a window.

Built-in bookcases provide much-needed storage in a home office and keep reference materials, computer equipment, etc. neat and convenient. Consider natural wood bookcases, as they give a home office a distinguished look, like an old English library. Configure them around a window to make the most of a wall that's already broken up.

Invest in a cozy reading nook.

Consider having a contractor build a window seat under a window to create a sunny reading nook.

Tie a red ribbon around your office doorknob.

Tie a red ribbon around your doorknob to help attract good luck to you and your business.

Create a U-shaped work surface.

Keep everything at your fingertips. A U-shaped desk provides lots of convenient work surface that you can easily access without ever having to get up from your chair.

Choose track lighting.

Instead of overhead fluorescents, use track lighting that lets you adjust individual lamps and focus light on specific work areas as needed.

Wash the windows in your office.

According to the principles of feng shui, windows symbolize the eyes. To see business or financial situations more clearly, wash the windows in your office.

Chapter Two:
SUMMER

Fill cracks in wood entrance doors.

Cracks in wood doors leak an unbelievable amount of air.
Luckily, they're easy to fix. Work from inside the room. On
painted doors, fill the cracks with wood filler or caulk. On
stained doors, use tinted wood putty. Then sand the area and
touch up the paint or stain.

Mix and match stair spindles.

Instead of opting for symmetry, combine several different spindle designs on your stair railing. It's more interesting. Alternate rope turned spindles with spool patterns, for instance.

Hang a wind chime in your entryway to circulate energy.

One way to circulate positive energy is to hang a wind chime in your entryway. The pleasing sound of the chimes will break up stuck energy and allow it to move more freely into other parts of your home.

Block drafts with a door sweep.

Without a door sweep to block it, cold air can easily swoop between the bottom of an entry door and the threshold. To replace or add a door sweep, start by measuring the door so you can buy one that fits. Next, tack or tape the sweep in place on the inside of the door, positioning it to touch the floor but not interfere with the door's ability to open and close. Drill pilot holes and drive screws to hold the sweep in place.

Decorate your entrance with all five Chinese elements.

To establish immediately a sense of balance and harmony in your home, include all five Chinese elements in your entry area. One way to do this is to place a mirror (water) with a brass (metal) frame above a rectangular (wood) hall table and set a ceramic (earth) vase of red (fire) flowers on the table.

Hang nine pictures in a long hallway.

Nine is the number of fulfillment and it's considered lucky in China, so this tip will attract good luck to your home. Choose pictures that depict positive scenes or represent your intentions.

Move your houseplants so they don't sit directly on a carpet or rug.

Set plants on a plastic or clay saucer, preferably on linoleum or hard wood that's easy to wipe clean. Even better, place the saucers on a small platform with rollers so you can just roll them a few feet when you need to clean. Otherwise, excess moisture from overwatering or simple condensation will form mildew on the carpet, which is hard to clean and a powerful irritant to allergy sufferers.

Use peach in your living room to attract luck and love.

Peach, which combines pink with yellow (the color of optimism and creativity), is also a good choice to include in your decorating scheme. In China, peach is linked with luck in love—the term "peach blossom luck" refers to someone who easily attracts romantic partners. If your intent is to bring new companions into your life, use peach in your living room's color scheme.

Choose cork floors to reduce noise.

Cork tiles, made from natural bark, dull the din in busy areas. Install a durable and handsome cork floor in your living room to muffle noise.

Configure seating in "conversation groups."

Interior designers arrange sofas and chairs in conversation groups so that people seated there can talk to one another without shouting. Try to position seating so that no one is more than about eight feet away from anyone else, and group furniture in an L, U, semicircular, or parallel configuration to facilitate conversation and camaraderie.

Use task lighting for special functions.

Task lighting shines on a specific spot so you can see to perform a particular task—a reading lamp could serve this purpose.

Use green in your living room to enhance prosperity.

Green is also the color of paper money in some cultures. In the West, we associate green with the earth element, which represents material goods and money. Including green in your decorating scheme can help increase prosperity, especially when used in the living room.

Consider installing a wooden ceiling.

Bead board isn't just for wainscoting. Affixed onto a ceiling, it adds visual interest while concealing cracks, watermarks, or other damage.

Place a jade Buddha in your living room.

In both Eastern and Western traditions, jade is associated with good health, prosperity, and well-being. To attract the good things in life, place a jade Buddha—preferably a laughing Buddha—in a prominent spot in your living room.

Consider opening up a ceiling.

A small, single-story ranch or bungalow can be more spacious if you open up a ceiling—or part of it—into the attic area. If structural beams/joists are needed, leave them exposed and integrate them as an attractive design feature.

Choose plants with round or curved leaves for your living room.

Plants with rounded leaves can encourage cooperation and unity among loved ones.

Dress up your windows.

Hang a decorative cornice or pediment above a door or window to dress it up. Consider molded plaster, carved wood, wrought iron, or a painting done on an arched panel as an attractive accent in a spot that's usually ignored.

Use thick rugs to promote a sense of security.

Thick, plushy, or nubby fabrics represent the earth element, whose qualities are security, warmth, and comfort. To emphasize these features in your social or family life, choose thick rugs that symbolize a sound, stable foundation underfoot.

Hang artwork at eye level.

The center of a painting should be at your eye level—not halfway between the back of the sofa and the ceiling. If you're hanging several pictures in a grouping, the center of the arrangement should be at eye level.

Use fabric patterned with wavy lines to promote cooperation.

Wavy lines are linked with flexibility and receptivity. To promote cooperation among family members and neighbors, use fabrics or wall coverings patterned with wavy lines or shapes (such as flowers, vines, swirls, spirals, or ripples) in your living room.

Take aim at switch-plate grime.

Get the grime—not the surrounding wall—when you're
cleaning a light-switch plate. Take an extra 10 minutes to cut
a cardboard frame to put around the light-switch plate before
you clean it. That will keep cleaning solution off your precious
wall or wallpaper.

Include deep green in your decorating scheme to promote serenity.

Green, a color that symbolizes plants, has a soothing effect on us and makes us feel calm and peaceful. The darker shades especially remind us of the shadowy depths of the forest or the ocean. To encourage a sense of serenity among friends or family members, include deep green in your living room's decorating scheme.

Backlight your plants.

Here's an easy way to add variety to your lighting scheme: Place spotlights on the floor behind large floor plants and direct the beams upward, so they shine on the ceiling. The light glowing through the leaves gives the impression of sunlight through trees.

Use your lamps with purpose.

If your goal is to stabilize your finances, choose a lamp with a metal or ceramic base. If you want to increase your prosperity, a wooden base is preferable. A lamp with a red base can bring you good luck. A lamp with a black base can help attract prosperity.

Place a vase of red flowers in your living room.

In China, red is considered a lucky color. To encourage good fortune in family and social matters, place a vase of red flowers in your living room. Be sure to trim or remove flowers as soon as they start to fade.

Burn floral-scented candles in your living room.

To promote feelings of affection and camaraderie among friends or family members, burn candles scented with essential oils of rose, gardenia, ylang-ylang, bergamot, sweet orange, or jasmine.

Choose an oval table to promote easy growth.

An oval combines the properties of a circle and a rectangle. If you wish to encourage growth in an area of your family or social life, or you'd like to improve your health or financial situation, an oval table can help you achieve your goals more gradually and gently than a rectangle will.

Use warm tones in the dining room.

Red, orange, and yellow stimulate the appetite, so these colors are good choices for a dining room or kitchen.

Be bold.

Don't be afraid to paint walls bright or dark colors—even in a small room, strong colors create a dramatic effect. Worst case scenario, you'll have to repaint.

Use a glass-topped dining table to spark pleasant conversation.

According to the Chinese principles of feng shui, glass is linked with the water element, whose beneficial qualities include cooperation, receptivity, and communication. If your goal is to enjoy pleasant intellectual exchanges at dinner, furnish your dining room with a glass-topped table.

Paint your dining room walls peach.

Peach combines the qualities of yellow, red, and white to bring good luck, optimism, and stability in areas associated with the dining room. Because peach is a mildly stimulating color, it piques the appetite and is an ideal choice for your dining room.

Decorate your ceiling.

Old mansions often featured ornate ceiling medallions in the dining room, from which a chandelier might have hung. Decorative medallions cast in synthetic materials are easy to install and instantly turn a drab ceiling into a showpiece.

Combine all five Chinese elements in your dining room to establish balance.

To create a sense of balance and harmony, include all five Chinese elements in your dining room. For example, use a glass-topped (water) table with a metal base (metal), select four (earth) chairs, and place a rectangular (wood) table over an Oriental rug that has red or orange (fire) in its design underneath the table.

Consider adding a chair rail.

Dining room walls come to life when you add a decorative wooden chair rail. The railing not only protects paint or wallpaper, it divides the walls into upper and lower sections to create extra interest. You could paint the upper portion and wallpaper the lower half, or hang bead board wainscoting below the chair rail and wallpaper the upper wall.

Set the mood with mood lighting.

Mood lighting acts to accent a room or offer a soft background glow when bright lights aren't appropriate. Use low-wattage lamps, wall sconces, chandeliers with candlelight bulbs, or torchieres to create this effect.

Purchase all the carpeting you need from the same dye lot.

If you want your carpeting to match perfectly, buy it all at the same time from the same dye lot. Carpet from a different dye lot may be slightly different in color. Check the lot numbers to make sure.

Always keep a vase of fresh flowers on your dining room table.

Place a vase of fresh flowers on your dining room table to connect diners with nature and to inspire positive feelings.

Arrange for flexible lighting.

Dimmer switches give you the best of all worlds. Use them
with lamps and overhead fixtures so you can shift from
ambient to task to mood lighting at the touch of a finger.
Choose from lots of different dimmer designs that are less
obtrusive than the old, knob-like switches.

Serve food on black dishes.

In China, black is considered a fortunate color where money
is concerned. Eating from black dishes can inspire financial
good luck.

Bring carpet samples home.

Before you purchase carpeting, bring samples home so you can see them in your own environment. The lighting in the store probably won't be the same as that in your home. View the samples at various times of the day, in natural and artificial light.

Keep clutter from piling up on your dining table.

If you don't eat in the dining room on a regular basis, the table may become a dumping zone. Clutter in the dining room can lead to confusion or upsets among household members or with social contacts. Keep your table free of clutter at all times, whether you eat in the dining room or not.

Avoid using your dining table as a desk or workstation.

Often the dining room ends up doing double duty as a workstation. Because work is incompatible with the social aspects of dining, try to avoid turning your dining table into a desk. If you don't have another option, at least clear the table of work-related materials before eating, and keep the area neat and clutter-free.

Position four chairs around the table to increase stability.

The number four is linked with security and permanence. To help stabilize your finances, family relationships, or social contacts, place four chairs around your dining table.

Put something red in your kitchen for good luck.

In China, red is considered lucky. To attract good fortune to your home, include red in your kitchen's decorating scheme.

Run major appliances at night.

Appliances, such as the dishwasher, generate heat when they're operating. At any time of year, it's cheaper to run these appliances at night after the outdoor temperature has dropped. On a cool summer night, your air conditioner won't have to work as hard to overcome a running appliance as it would during the day. On a frigid winter night, the heat of a running appliance will give your heating system a little extra help.

Give your dishwasher a pretty face.

Many manufacturers of kitchen cabinets offer matching fronts for dishwashers. Cover up your dishwasher with panels that let it blend in with your cabinets.

Choose quartz countertops for durable beauty.

Made from natural quartz crystal, these countertops are more durable and easier to care for than granite. They require no sealing or polishing and resist stains from red wine, coffee, tea, tomato juice, and other substances that can damage the finish on granite. Here's another idea to consider: Although manufacturers make no claims to the metaphysical properties of quartz countertops, many energy workers and healers use quartz crystals to clear, strengthen, and balance the body's vital energy field. It's possible that quartz countertops could have a positive effect on your energy, too.

Keep passageways through your kitchen free of clutter and obstacles.

From a practical standpoint, cluttered walkways in your kitchen might pose health or safety risks. From the perspective of the Chinese principles of feng shui, clutter obstructs the smooth flow of chi, thereby hampering the flow of health and wealth into your life. Clear the traffic patterns through your kitchen to enhance your physical and financial well-being.

Cook with gas—and electricity.

Many cooks like the versatility and effectiveness of dual-fuel ranges. Consider upgrading your old stove to one that combines an electric oven with a gas-fired cook top.

Save counter space with a drawer-style microwave.

Instead of taking up room on your countertop, a microwave oven in a drawer can be installed under the countertop. It's convenient, yet out-of-the way.

Use gold in your decorating scheme to attract wealth.

Because the Chinese principles of feng shui connects the kitchen with wealth, you can increase your money-drawing power by using the color gold in your kitchen. Bright golden tones also remind us of the sun's life-giving energy and therefore increase optimism. Paint your kitchen walls a sunny yellow-gold to boost prosperity and happiness.

Consider that two drawers are better than one.

Dishwashers with two separate washing compartments are ideal for small households and people on the go who don't cook or eat home very much. Because you can fill only one section at a time with dishes and run the equivalent of half an ordinary load, two-drawer dishwashers save energy and water. Another plus: Dual washing controls let you run two loads at once and adjust the individual cleaning cycles to suit your needs. Fill one drawer with pots and pans, the other with glasses.

Make your appliances sparkle.

Remove fingerprints, watermarks, food stains, and other unsightly marks from stainless steel appliances with WD-40. Pour a little on a soft cloth and wipe stainless steel surfaces with it to clean and protect your appliances.

Nix the garbage disposal.

If your home has a septic system instead of being hooked up to a city sewer line, a garbage disposal may not be a good idea. The bacteria that keep the septic tank operating effectively don't process uneaten food, so pouring veggie scraps and ground up eggshells into your system may overtax it. Consider composting instead. You can use the rich soil to nourish your plants.

Consider using track lighting in kitchen work areas.

Adjustable track lighting allows you to shine light where you need it most. Easy to install and inexpensive, track lighting is more attractive than florescent fixtures and more flexible than recessed canisters. Small-scale units with high-intensity halogen lights work well even in kitchens with low ceilings.

Use orange to stimulate appetite.

Studies show that fiery colors, particularly orange, tend to stimulate appetite, so this is an ideal hue to use in the kitchen. If bright orange is too strong for your taste, try peach, apricot, or terra-cotta instead. Or incorporate a few flame-orange accents into your kitchen's décor.

Choose a single-lever faucet set.

A single-lever faucet lets you adjust water temperature and velocity easily with one hand. Unless you want an authentic, retro, or old-fashioned look, a single-lever kitchen faucet is usually more convenient than dual hot-and-cold handles.

Avoid curtains in a kitchen.

Kitchens look brighter, neater, and more spacious when windows are left bare. In a busy kitchen, curtains will require frequent washing and ironing to keep them looking fresh and pretty. If privacy is an issue, replace curtains with easy-care mini-blinds. If you don't need privacy, eliminate window treatments altogether.

Choose black appliances to encourage prosperity.

In China, black is considered the color of wealth. Therefore, it's a good color to include in your kitchen. Black appliances—especially the stove, which generates wealth—can help you attract prosperity.

Choose solid surface countertops for seamless beauty.

Solid surface countertops, such as Corian, can be fabricated so there are no visible seams at joints—an advantage over granite or quartz countertops. Although not as hard and scratch-resistant as stone, these surfaces can be sanded and repaired if they get damaged.

Go wild in a small bathroom.

Small baths and powder rooms can be fun places to really let your imagination soar. Select bright paint colors, faux finishes, or way-out wallpaper to make this oft-overlooked space distinctive.

Choose colored bathroom fixtures to minimize maintenance.

Some water supplies contain minerals or other substances that can stain tubs, toilets, and sinks. Lime in the water, for instance, leaves a greenish residue on porcelain and plastic. If iron is present in your water, choose red, brown, or black fixtures to prevent unsightly rust marks. Replace old white porcelain with new colors that hide stains.

Make an antique mirror a focal point.

Instead of hanging an ordinary bathroom vanity mirror, dress up your bathroom with a unique, antique mirror above the sink, perhaps one that was designed originally to hang over a buffet or dresser. Choose one with a frame of carved wood or ornate gilt. If you're creative, you may enjoy painting the frame with flowers, geometric designs, or a faux stone finish. Or set mirrored glass into a handsome old picture frame.

Have GFCI electrical outlets installed in your bathroom.

GFCI, or ground fault circuit interrupter electrical outlets, reduce the risk of electrocution. Have them installed above the bathroom sink, outside the shower, etc. Building codes in some areas require GFCIs instead of ordinary electrical outlets to be used near any water source.

Replace the bathtub sealant.

It takes only a few minutes to repair old sealant around your bathtub. Cracked, mildew-caked sealant and grout are not only unsightly, the decomposition can allow moisture to seep behind the tub and cause more serious problems. Scrape out old grout, then squeeze a line of silicone around the joint between your tub and tile surround. Wipe away excess and let dry overnight.

Keep toilet lids down.

Guys, here's an incentive to remember to put that toilet seat down. According to the Chinese principles of feng shui, energy (or chi) seeps away from your home via the drains. To prevent the loss of chi, keep toilet lids closed.

Invest in a water-saving toilet.

Flushing the toilet accounts for approximately one-quarter of all indoor water usage. Older toilets use about five to seven gallons of water per flush, compared with about one-and-a-half gallons for modern water-saving models. Many communities' building codes require that low-flow toilets be installed in new homes and when a bathroom is remodeled. Replace your antiquated, wasteful toilet with a more efficient one. The net savings could be as much as 20,000 gallons of water per toilet per year.

Set a live plant on the toilet tank.

Placing a live plant on the tank counteracts the draining effect of the toilet. Chi is drawn to the plant's positive energy instead of slipping away down the drain.

Repair a leaky toilet.

About 20 percent of all toilets leak, wasting water and money. Sometimes the solution is as simple as adjusting the float on the toilet's refill valve. Or the stopper may be getting hung up, rather than settling properly to stop water flow from the tank. Fixing a leak could save you a couple hundred gallons of water per day.

Use one color on your walls and ceilings.

Especially if you're using a light shade, paint the walls and ceiling the same color. This "wrap-around" technique saves time. You don't have to carefully cut in where the walls and ceiling join.

Place matching nightstands on either side of the bed.

The number two signifies partnership and harmony. To encourage feelings of togetherness and cooperation, place a pair of matching nightstands on either side of your bed.

Position the bed so that when your child is in it, she can see the room's entrance.

Position children's beds so that when they are in bed, they can easily view the door to the room. This placement provides comfort and security, because it allows children to see immediately anyone who enters their rooms.

Put kids' dirty clothes in a hamper.

Put a hamper in every bedroom closet. Train your kids to drop their dirty clothes in their hamper, not on the floor, bed, chairs, and every other available surface.

Use red in your decorating scheme to spark passion.

We connect red with passion and vitality, so it's a good color to use in your master bedroom if you want to turn up the heat in a romantic relationship. Because red is a stimulating color, it may be too strong to use in large doses, however, as it could interfere with restful sleep. You can also use red flowers, a big red heart, red throw pillows, or a picture in a red frame.

Arrange special photos on a fabric memo board and hang it on the wall.

No one has enough space to frame every picture they would like to. A great way to maximize your family picture display is to use a fabric memo board. Stick some favorite pictures under the ribbons, and you can easily change them whenever you're inspired!

Choose a wall to accent with color.

Choose one wall—perhaps the headboard wall or the wall you see first when you wake up in the morning—to paint in a bold accent color. You might want to experiment with decorative glazes, sponge or rag painting, stenciling, or even a mural.

Avoid switching paint cans when painting a wall.

If a room will require more than one gallon of paint, complete as many entire walls as possible from one gallon. When you near the bottom of the can, begin a new wall with a new gallon. Don't paint part of a wall from one can, then expect the paint in another can to match. Even if they were purchased at the same time, the color mix might not be exactly the same in both cans.

Place matching lamps on either side of the bed.

To increase the positive energy in a primary partnership or to brighten your romantic prospects, place a pair of matching lamps in your master bedroom, one on either side of the bed.

Save some paint for touchups.

Save a small amount of paint for touchups, but dispose of it after a year. By then the color on your walls will have faded or discolored slightly.

Use pink in your decorating scheme to encourage loving feelings.

Pink is associated with romance, affection, and joy. Use pink in your master bedroom to attract love and happiness in a primary partnership.

Use a round area rug to promote cooperation and harmony.

Because circles symbolize union and wholeness, they can encourage children to cooperate with others. Place a round area rug in a child's bedroom to promote feelings of peace, harmony, and togetherness. This is especially important if two or more children share the same bedroom or if sibling rivalry exists in your home. Try to position furniture so that each piece rests partly on the rug to create a sense of unity.

Design a color scheme around a favorite piece of fabric.

Start with a bedspread, curtain fabric, Oriental rug, or other patterned piece of material and base your color scheme on it. Use colors on walls, carpets, etc. in the same proportions as they are shown on your favorite piece of fabric.

Install a pegboard at "kid height."

Make it easy for kids to hang up their clothes and keep their rooms neat. Install pegboards at a height that's convenient for them to reach. Adjust clothing rods in children's closets to a convenient height, too.

Tie a nine-inch-long red ribbon on your bedroom's doorknob.

This tip combines two lucky symbols: the color red and the number nine. Tie the ribbon on the doorknob of your master bedroom to attract good luck and invite love into your life.

Provide open shelving for toys and games.

Open shelving provides an easy place for kids to put toys and games away when they're finished playing with them, and it helps keep clutter at bay.

Periodically rearrange the furniture.

Whenever you change something in your home, you stimulate change in your life. Because children change so quickly, it's a good idea to rearrange the furniture in their bedrooms periodically—say, every six months or so—to keep pace with their growth and inspire them to continue evolving. If a child is experiencing anxiety in connection with frequent or stressful life changes, however, you can help balance the upsets by leaving furniture in the same place for a longer period.

Paint your bedroom peach to attract new love.

In China, the color peach is believed to attract romance—
the term "peach blossom luck" refers to someone who is
lucky in love. If you want to begin a new relationship, paint
your bedroom peach.

Prominently hang a calendar that clearly lists chores.

It's never too early to get your children organized! Kids need a sense of order in their lives—it gives them a sense of stability. Make a calendar with everyone's name and chores in different colors of ink.

Replace drapes with shutters.

Ideal for homes with country or casual décor, louvered
wooden shutters are inexpensive and easy to install.
Adjustable louvers also allow you to vary the amount of light
and privacy you desire. Shutters give an airy, uncluttered
appearance in a small room, too.

Position furniture so it doesn't block doors or windows.

According to the Chinese principles of feng shui, energy enters your home via the doors and windows. If, when you open a door, you bump a piece of furniture, chi will be blocked and your social life could suffer. Arrange furniture in your office so that it doesn't interfere with the free flow of chi.

Use a round or oval rug to encourage congeniality.

Circles are ancient, universal symbols of unity and harmony. To promote unity, peace, and happiness among your business contacts, put a round or oval rug in your office.

Use plastic sheet covers to preserve special artwork or letters, and store them in a separate binder for each child.

Kids put a great deal of effort into making pictures and writing cards. Shouldn't you put a little effort into keeping them intact? Put special pieces in clear plastic sheet covers and file them in a binder to keep these memories organized.

Pay attention to the areas where clutter collects.

Clutter represents confusion, upsets, obstacles, and stress. Notice which areas tend to become cluttered in your office— these may indicate the parts of your business or life that are unsettled or causing problems. By clearing away the clutter and organizing your belongings, you can help bring order and clarity to your work.

Use gilt frames to attract money.

Gilt (gold-colored paint) represents wealth and luxury—use gilt frames for artwork if you want to improve your finances.

Choose furniture with curved lines to promote harmony.

Curved lines and circles are ancient, universal symbols of unity and congeniality. To encourage cooperation and harmony with business associates or contacts, choose office furnishings with curved lines, such as French country, Queen Anne, or Victorian styles.

Chapter Three:
FALL

Hang a photo of household members in the foyer.

This introduces visitors to the people who live in your home. It also gives anyone who enters your home a sense of being greeted by household members and welcomed into your living space.

Paint or seal your wood doors.

Unless all the edges of a wood door are finished, it expands and contracts with the weather, which encourages cracks to form. To prevent this from happening, paint or seal all the edges of the door—including the top and bottom. You can find high-quality wood sealers in the parts department of a hardware store or home center, or at any paint retailer.

Put a piece of jade in your entrance area.

Jade is linked with good health, prosperity, and well-being. Put a chunk of tumbled jade or, better yet, an attractive figurine made of jade in your entryway. This invites good fortune to bless relatives and neighbors who come into your home.

Remember where you come in.

It's fine to keep a grand entrance up front, complete with scrubbed porch and polished railings, but if everyone enters through, say, the kitchen or side door, that's where you should concentrate your cleaning efforts. Be especially sure to put a doormat wherever the people you consider family enter the house, and shake it out and/or sweep under it at least once a week.

Give the front door a once-over with Windex.

A quick spruce-up at the entrance requires little more than Windex and a cloth. Windex gives a fast sparkle to chrome, glass, and most metal fixtures.

Create a focal point in your entry area.

Help visitors get their bearings when they enter your home by creating an attractive focal point for them to look at—a large healthy plant, an appealing picture or sculpture, or a handsome piece of furniture.

Place six objects on a hall table.

According to the Chinese principles of feng shui, six is the number of give-and-take and encourages cooperation. When visitors or household members enter your home, they subconsciously register this number and its symbolism. Use objects that represent your intentions or that have positive associations for you.

Hang a mirror on an obstructing wall.

When you enter your home, do you immediately encounter a wall? If so, you have undoubtedly experienced the sensation of being blocked or stopped by this obstruction. To alleviate this condition, hang a mirror on the wall. The mirror symbolically cuts a hole or window in the wall, thereby opening up the confined space.

Burn spicy-scented candles in your living room.

To spark lively intellectual exchanges and stimulate enthusiasm among friends or family members, burn candles scented with spicy aromas, such as cinnamon, clove, ginger, cedar, sandalwood, or patchouli.

Position sofas and chairs so no one's back faces the door.

Arrange sofas and chairs in your living room so that when seated, no one will have his or her back to the entrance. This configuration welcomes people into the room and prevents those who are already seated from being startled by someone coming up behind them.

Let a favorite painting inspire your color scheme.

Can't decide on a color scheme? Let the great masters guide you. Flip through art books until you find a painting you like and examine the way the artist has combined colors in his/her composition. Van Gogh's "Starry Night," for example, emphasizes blues and indigos, with smaller amounts of buttery yellow and mustard. Follow the artist's lead and use the same color palette for your walls, carpeting, upholstery, and accessories.

Reflect the culture of your community.

In your remodeling and/or decorating scheme, bring in some themes from a prominent culture in your community. If you live in the Southwest, for instance, American Indian or Mexican elements could add interest to your home. Pennsylvania Dutch motifs could brighten a home in Pennsylvania; Celtic imagery might work well in Boston.

Select three hues for your color scheme.

Here's a tried-and-true formula for creating successful color schemes: Use three different hues in the following proportions: 60 percent of the main color, 30 percent of the second color, and 10 percent of an accent color.

Something old, something new.

Mix and match elements from different time periods, blending old with new to create interest. A Victorian stained glass window could add color to a sleek, modern bathroom. An Art Deco floor lamp could be handsome next to a contemporary Italian sofa.

Divide and conquer.

Wide open spaces can seem impersonal and hard to "tame." Divide a great room or family room into two or more sections to scale them down and make them easier to decorate. Think about possible ways you and household members might use the space, then create a conversation area, a private reading area, an area for games, etc.

Pick an accent color for woodwork.

Instead of the customary off-white woodwork, choose a
distinctive color for the trim in your room—especially if you're
blessed with decorative crown moldings, wainscoting, dental
moldings, or other interesting details. Try peach woodwork
with taupe walls or dark green trim with creamy yellow walls.

Place a bookcase in your living room.

If you'd like to attract intelligent, literary companions or
emphasize learning and communication among family
members, place a bookcase in your living room.

Add columns to define your space.

Decorative columns visually divide and define sections of your living space. They also add a touch of grandeur. Hint: Don't skimp—choose columns that are large enough and distinctive enough to make a statement.

Choose a split complementary color scheme for your living room.

This popular color scheme uses three hues to attract good luck and establish a sense of harmony in your living environment. Use a color wheel that shows the primary, secondary, and tertiary colors. Select a color you like as your principal hue. Then find its complement (the color directly opposite it on the wheel). The two hues on either side of the complementary color are the ones to use in conjunction with your main color. For example, combine yellow (main color) with magenta and blue-violet.

Burn incense to stimulate communication and congeniality.

Incense combines the Western elements of air and fire, which are linked with communication and enthusiasm respectively. In some spiritual traditions, incense is burned to send messages and prayers to deities. To attract cheerful companions with whom you can enjoy lively conversation and good times, burn incense in your living room.

Don't let magazines and newspapers clutter up your living room.

Clutter in your living room symbolizes confusion in relationships with friends or family members. Magazines and newspapers are prime sources of clutter—as soon as you've read them, recycle them or pass them along. If you're in a hurry and don't have time to clean up paper clutter, at least straighten the piles of magazines and newspapers so they look neat.

Keep closet doors closed.

Closets represent private areas of your life. If your living room has a closet, make sure you keep the door closed so guests aren't privy to your "secrets."

Use a phoenix to increase your power.

The legendary phoenix (think Harry Potter!) is rich with symbolism—it represents power and triumph over adversity. Display a picture of a phoenix in your living room to help you increase personal power and remove obstacles to happiness.

Periodically rearrange the furniture in your living room.

To prevent stagnation, move the furniture in your living room around at least once each year. By changing your furniture arrangement, you symbolically invite new people and experiences into your life.

Display family photos in your living room.

Displaying photos of family members in your living room demonstrates your desire for congenial relationships with loved ones.

Ring a bell to chase away bad vibes.

Ring a bell when you enter the living room. The pleasing sound breaks up stale energy and helps chase away bad vibes. Ring the bell once in each corner of the room and once in the center to stimulate positive energy.

Choose a square table to ensure stability and security.

Squares offer stability. If you're trying to create a more secure, permanent home situation or want to stabilize your finances, health, or social structure, choose a square dining table.

Sponge-paint your walls.

Sponging is one of the easiest and fastest of all decorative painting techniques. The unique, textured look hides minor imperfections in walls and adds drama to your room.

Remember to leave a little room at the top.

You'll get a cleaner-looking line and avoid getting paint on the ceiling if you leave about ⅛- to ¼-inch (5 to 8 mm) at the top of the walls instead of painting all the way up to where they join the ceiling. You can do this only if the old color is close to the ceiling color, for instance, white over off-white walls. If you're doing blue over red it won't work very well. Hint: This sounds obvious, but always paint the ceiling first.

Choose a wooden table to promote growth.

As with rectangular objects, furniture made from wood encourages expansion. Choose a wooden table for your dining room if you'd like your family or your social circle to grow.

Choose flat paint when hiding imperfections.

Flat paint does a better job of concealing minor imperfections on walls and woodwork. The glossier the paint, the more those little irregularities will stand out.

Dress up your switch plates.

Replace ordinary plastic switch plates with decorative ones—metal, leather, porcelain, wood—that reflect your décor or personality.

Use green in your dining room's décor.

Green offers many positive associations, making it an ideal color for a dining room. It compliments most foods and reminds us of leafy vegetables, thus it promotes good health. A soothing yin color, it encourages diners to feel serene and facilitates digestion.

Place two candles in silver or brass candleholders.

To strengthen or solidify a romantic relationship, put two candles in silver or brass candleholders on your dining room table. Two is the number of partnership; the metal element provides structure and permanence.

Use images of horses to improve your health.

In China, horses represent longevity. In the West, we associate horses with power, freedom, and vitality. Tap into this positive symbolism by displaying a picture or sculpture of a horse in your dining room.

Mist your dining room with a fresh scent.

To clear the air and promote mental clarity, mist your dining room with a fresh, clean scent that's mildly stimulating. Citrus and mint are good choices.

Position six chairs around the table to encourage give-and-take.

Six is the number of give-and-take. To promote positive interpersonal exchange, cooperation, and sharing among household members, place six chairs around your dining room table.

Use triangles to stimulate change.

This geometric shape corresponds to the fire element and suggests movement or change. Because a triangle has three points, it is also linked with the number three, which the Chinese consider lucky. Display a triangular-shaped object in your dining room or use fabric with triangles, flame-shaped designs, or zigzags to spark change.

Turn off the TV while eating.

TV can be a disruptive influence at mealtime. Watching programs that feature violence (such as the evening news) can upset digestion or exacerbate conflict between diners. Even upbeat shows distract diners from each other and interfere with the social aspects of sharing a meal.

Give each diner his or her own candle.

Rather than using a candelabra or pair of candlesticks on your dining table, set a small votive candle at each person's place.

Choose white appliances to promote stability in your home.

The Chinese connect white with the metal element, which provides stability and structure. To enhance your family's sense of order, permanence, and structure, choose white appliances for your kitchen.

Consider replacing a double sink with a single one.

Standard double sinks usually aren't big enough to wash large pots and pans. A single, large sink that's at least 15" (30 cm) deep may be a more practical choice.

Tie a red ribbon around your faucet for good luck.

Red is considered a lucky color in China. To attract good fortune into your home, tie a red ribbon around your kitchen faucet. Each time you turn on the tap, you'll be reminded of your goal to increase your luck.

Invest in high-quality faucets.

Inexpensive faucets may not blend hot and cold water evenly. Usually higher-end faucets contain more effective mixing chambers that allow you to better control water temperature and pressure.

Clean clogged drains naturally.

Combine ½ cup (36 g) baking soda and ½ cup (118 ml) white vinegar, then pour the mixture down the drain. Next, pour a pot of boiling water down the drain to dissolve blockages caused by food particles, soap, and grease.

Install a water conditioning unit.

Minerals in your water supply can damage plumbing and shorten the life span of dishwashers, water heaters, and other appliances. If you have hard water in your home, consider using a water conditioning system.

Choose colorful appliances to brighten a kitchen.

Although white, black, bisque, and stainless steel still dominate the field, appliances in cheerful colors are making a comeback. Stoves and refrigerators in yellow, red, blue, or green can add drama to your kitchen.

Paint your refrigerator.

If your refrigerator is still in good condition, but the old finish doesn't match your new kitchen's color scheme, give it a facelift. For significantly less than the cost of a new fridge you can have your old one professionally resurfaced right in your home.

Allow space on either side of your stove.

The stove generates wealth, but if it is crammed into a corner of your kitchen its money-drawing power will be limited. If possible, position your stove so there's plenty of counter space on either side. If this isn't possible, hang a small mirror on the enclosed side to open up the area symbolically.

Choose a refrigerator with a freezer at the bottom.

Although refrigerators with freezers on the bottom tend to be more expensive than those with the freezer at the top, the extra cost may be justified by their extra convenience. Bottom-freezer models put the foods and drinks you use most often where they're easy to see and reach, without bending over.

Change the way a refrigerator door opens.

Refrigerators doors come assembled with the handles on the left. If you want the doors to swing the other way, say so when you purchase your fridge. The store from which you purchase it can make the adjustment before the fridge is delivered. (If you're handy with tools, it's easy to change the door yourself.)

Know that two ovens are better than one.

Whether you choose a free-standing range or a built-in wall model, two ovens are better than one. People who like to cook can bake a pie in one oven and roast a turkey in the other. People who rarely cook big meals can use the smaller oven most of the time and save energy.

Hang "top-down, bottom-up" shades.

Shades and blinds that can be lowered to allow light in at the top or raised to let light in at the bottom provide maximum versatility. Install them in your kitchen to give just the right amount of light and privacy.

Choose vinyl flooring for economic practicality.

Whether you opt for squares or sheets, vinyl flooring offers practicality and affordability. With an extensive range of available colors, patterns, and textures, vinyl flooring is compatible with virtually any kitchen style. Self-adhesive vinyl squares are easy to apply; sheet vinyl requires a bit more skill.

Prevent clutter from piling up on your countertops.

Not only is clutter unsightly, but it can also pose health and safety hazards when it accumulates on your kitchen countertops. Clutter also represents confusion, stress, and obstacles—in your kitchen, this can translate into health or money problems. Keep your countertops free of clutter for practical reasons as well as symbolic ones.

Make sure your kitchen door opens easily.

In many homes, the kitchen door is the one most frequently used. Therefore, this is where chi enters your living space. If the door sticks or can't be opened completely, chi will have a hard time getting inside to energize your home. Adjust the door so it opens and closes easily and clear away any obstructions that block it.

Clean out your refrigerator regularly.

Make a point of cleaning out your refrigerator weekly. Not only is spoiled food a health risk, it also symbolizes waste and old, unwanted stuff that no longer has a place in your life.

Mist your kitchen with citrus scent.

The fresh, clean scent of citrus can clear the air in your kitchen—literally and figuratively. Lemon, lime, orange, and grapefruit aromas also stimulate the mind and refresh your spirit. Pour a few drops of essential oil into a bottle of water and periodically mist your kitchen with the mixture.

Leave some elbow room.

If you're placing the toilet next to a sink/vanity, make sure to leave enough elbow room between them. Eighteen inches (40 cm) from the edge of the sink or vanity to the center of the toilet is considered the minimum amount of space for personal comfort.

Replace washers in dripping faucets.

Leaky faucets not only waste water—and money—they can produce stains in your sink. Fix them in a few minutes by installing new washers. Hint: Washers comes in different sizes, so take the old one with you when you go to purchase a replacement.

Install a single-lever faucet in the shower.

Instead of separate hot and cold water handles, choose a single-lever model for your shower. It's easier to operate and safer, too. Building codes in some communities require single-lever faucets be used in bathrooms to reduce the risk of scalding.

Tie a gold ribbon around your showerhead to attract prosperity.

This simple cure reminds you to focus on prosperity while you shower. The gold ribbon symbolizes wealth, and falling water is a source of positive energy. Together, they represent blessings and abundance flowing down on you.

Put new handles on an old tub.

If the handles on an antique, claw-foot tub are rusted or dripping, it's easy to replace them. With a wrench, remove the old handles and stems. Before you attach the new handles, wrap the stems with plumber's tape and coat them with heat-resistant grease to help reduce wear and tear and extend their useful life.

Design a decorative tile shower stall.

Create a unique design for your shower on graph paper (make sure it's to scale), with each square representing a piece of colored tile. Mix and match solids and patterns; even render a landscape, mosaic, or other picture with tiles. When you're confident in your design, head to the home store to purchase the materials you'll need.

Tie a green ribbon around your showerhead to promote good health.

This tip helps you focus on your health and well-being whenever you shower. Imagine the falling water—which is a source of positive energy—washing away any impurities, illnesses, or other health problems. The green ribbon represents life, growth, and serenity.

Place two candles in your bedroom to promote togetherness.

This combines two symbolic feng shui cures: the fire element and the number two. Fire stimulates enthusiasm and passion, and the number two represents partnership and togetherness. Candlelight, as we all know, invites romance.

Clean out old shoes from the closet.

Kids quickly outgrow their shoes. Make sure your child's closet is filled with shoes that are the right size, so that his little toes don't get crunched!

Hang a mirror so that it reflects the guest room door.

If you can't situate the bed in the ideal place (in view of the room's entrance), hang a mirror on the wall so that when your guests are in bed, they can see the entrance reflected in the mirror. This allows them to see anyone who might enter the room and avoid surprises.

Remove items that might interfere with a guest's comfort.

Guest rooms often serve multiple purposes—they may double as home offices, workout rooms, or storage areas. To ensure your guests enjoy a comfortable, restful visit, remove items such as computers, exercise equipment, or hobby and craft supplies that might interfere with their comfort. If you can't relocate these items, consider covering or screening them from your guests' view.

Avoid ironing.

Yes, it's true: Ironing is expensive. In fact, in an average family, an iron consumes as much energy as a clothes washer doing five loads of laundry a week. So, here's your official permission—no, make that encouragement—to avoid ironing whenever possible. You might even want to invest in some of those new, no-iron cottons that come out of the dryer ready to wear.

Put all toys and balls in a toy box.

You can't have too many toy-storage areas! Kids need their own toy storage in their bedrooms, too. Put all toys into a nice toy box that matches their room's decor. Find a toy box that will grow with the kids—one that you can redecorate whenever you redecorate their room.

Don't let dirty laundry collect in your bedroom.

Energy gets stuck on dirt, resulting in stagnant conditions. Dirty laundry also represents unpleasant business and secrets—qualities that can damage a romantic partnership. Instead of using a clothes hamper in your master bedroom, put dirty clothes in a hall closet, bathroom, or other area of your home.

Provide space in a guest-room closet.

Guest-room closets frequently serve as additional storage
sites for family members' belongings. To make guests feel
welcome, however, clear a space in the closet for them to
hang their clothing. A full closet indicates there's no room for
anyone else in your home.

If your child has more than a couple of pairs of shoes, organize them in a shoe rack.

If your child is a budding fashion plate, you might want to put a shoe rack on the closet floor or hang one from the closet door. This way, she'll be able to see everything she has, and wear them before her feet grow again!

Keep your bedroom free of clutter.

Clutter represents confusion and attitudes or behaviors that can cause problems in a primary partnership. Clear clutter from your master bedroom to promote clarity and comfort in your love life.

Take down the curtains in a small bedroom.

Curtains and drapes visually enclose a room. To make a small space seem larger, eliminate bulky window treatments. Instead, opt for mini-blinds, shutters, or simple fabric shades set within the window frame.

Don't get stuck in symmetry.

You don't have to stick with matched bedroom sets. It's more fun to mix it up. In a child's bedroom or a guest room, use two different single beds instead of a pair, perhaps two different antique brass or iron headboards. Put different bedspreads on them, too. Unite the two by using the same colors.

Position the bed so you can see the door.

If you can see the entrance to your bedroom when you are
in bed, you'll feel secure and comfortable—no one can enter
without your knowledge. Place the bed so that it faces the
door, preferably in a spot that is as far away from the doorway
as possible.

Create a sanctuary in your home.

Set aside a quiet, private spot in your home where you can retreat to enjoy peace and quiet—an attic hideaway, a nap nook built into a large bay window niche, a meditation area nestled in an alcove under eaves, or a reading corner in the home office. Surround yourself with comfortable furnishings and personal treasures, things that make you feel nourished and secure. Let this private sanctuary be your own, special R&R getaway.

Place a piece of rose quartz on your desk.

Rose quartz emits gentle, pleasing vibrations that can promote harmony and ease. As a result, this semiprecious gemstone is often associated with love and affection. Place a smooth, tumbled chunk of rose quartz on your desk to encourage happiness in a business partnership.

Freshen carpets with baking soda.

Whether you need to pick up pet odors or merely want to freshen your carpet, try ordinary baking soda before turning to the chemical or highly scented stuff. Using a baking sifter, sprinkle baking soda liberally over the carpet and let it sit for about 20 minutes. When you vacuum up the baking soda, the smells and some of the fine dirt go with it.

Use an image of fish to attract prosperity.

If you don't want to install an aquarium, you can still use the lucky symbolism associated with fish to attract wealth and success.

Use black in your decorating scheme to increase prosperity.

Incorporating black, the Chinese color of wealth, into your office color scheme can help improve your prosperity. A black leather desk chair or black file cabinets are obvious choices, but a sleek black desk could be an attractive item, too.

Choose recessed ceiling lights for your home office.

Recessed canisters in your office ceiling, when positioned around the perimeter of the room, provide pleasant ambient light. Hint: Add dimmer switches so you can adjust light levels as needed.

Paint your office door green to increase prosperity.

Because green is the color of money in some countries, you can attract financial growth to your business by painting your office door green. In feng shui, green is considered an earth color and, as such, it encourages security, comfort, and stability in financial areas.

Corral your computer cords.

Use a piece of foam-tube insulation to tidy a mass of cords. Just cut a lengthwise slit in a piece about 6 inches (15 cm) long, nail or glue it below your desk, and feed the cords into the tube. Small, self-adhering clips that help guide and hold cords in place are also available at office-supply stores.

Use a black phone to encourage prosperous communication with colleagues and customers.

Black is considered a fortunate color in China, because it is associated with wealth. Using a black phone can help stimulate business and prosperity—especially if your work involves a lot of telephone contact. Salespeople, in particular, can benefit from this cure.

Consider carving out wall niches.

Wall niches—like those recessed alcoves in the walls of old missions and monasteries—are a great way to display statues, artifacts, and other treasures. They provide an interesting and attractive alternative to shelves for showcasing artwork.

Chapter Four:
WINTER

Illuminate your foyer adequately.

Have you ever entered a dark hallway or vestibule and felt uncomfortable, even anxious? A brightly lit foyer, on the other hand, invites you to enter—visitors instantly feel safe and welcome in your home.

Use a triangle to direct positive energy into your home.

To keep energy from languishing in your foyer, position a triangle so that it points toward the main part of your home. This symbol works like an arrow to direct positive energy into your living area.

Keep closet doors shut.

Because closets represent hidden or private matters, you'll want to keep the door shut on an entry area closet. This prevents your personal affairs from becoming public.

Try dim lighting.

Entryways often have harsh, unflattering lighting that shows
every cobweb and crayon mark on the wall. And strong light
in the living room or dining room is great to read by, but also
great to see dust by. Consider switching out a few white bulbs
in these areas for softer colors—pink or peach, for example, or
the warm (and kind) light of an amber bulb.

Choose warm colors.

If you live in a cold climate, warm up north-facing hallways or
entrances by painting them peach, yellow, pink, orange, or red.

Clear the passageways from your foyer into your living area.

Clear away any obstructions that inhibit easy movement from the foyer to the main part of your living area. Clutter, furniture, or architectural elements that jut into the walkways will block chi and make it difficult for you to move freely into your home.

Opt for cool colors.

Studies show that we respond physically as well as psychologically to the colors around us. If you live in a hot climate, paint south- and west-facing rooms green, blue, or gray to produce a cooling effect.

Put a cinnamon stick in the vacuum bag.

It will leave a homey odor in the air, not the musty smell the vacuum can put out.

Use a rectangular rug to expand your social network.

According to the Chinese principles of feng shui, rectangles are used to stimulate growth. If you want to expand your social network, meet new people, or encourage more interaction with friends and neighbors, place a rectangular area rug in your living room.

Expose a brick chimney.

In many older homes the chimney has been covered up with wallboard, plaster, or paneling. Hire someone to remove it. Old brick adds character to a room; expose it all the way up to the ceiling.

Keep walkways through your living room free of clutter and obstacles.

If the passageways through your living room are obstructed by furniture or clutter, good energy will have a hard time circulating. Make sure the walkways through your living room are free of obstacles.

For your living room, choose artwork that depicts people.

An empty landscape isn't the best choice for your living room—make sure there are people in the pictures you display in the social areas of your home. Otherwise, you're sending a message that you prefer a solitary existence.

Consider tiling around a fireplace opening.

Decorative tile is a great tool for dressing up a fireplace. Consider affixing handsome, fireproof ceramic tile to the masonry on the front of the fireplace's opening to give it a distinctive look and to cover minor cracks or other damage.

Hang three pictures in an area to stimulate change.

Is there something about your family or social life you'd like to change? One way to spark change is to hang three pictures. Be careful, though—change isn't always easy to control. Choose pictures that represent the situations you desire.

Use rectangular wooden picture frames to promote growth.

In China, wood and rectangles are associated with expansion. To encourage growth, frame artwork and photographs in wood.

Feeling down? Turn up the lights.

Turn up the lights on cold, dark days—it will make your home seem more open, cheerful, and inviting.

Choose a distinctive mantel.

Transform an ordinary fireplace into a dramatic focal point by adding a distinctive mantel. A mantelpiece made of marble or carved mahogany dresses up a traditional room. A hefty slab of mesquite, cedar, or oak adds a striking note to a rustic fieldstone fireplace. A simple shelf of granite or smoky glass makes a smart statement in a contemporary setting.

Hang a picture of a landscape to create the illusion of space.

Especially in a small room, a picture of a landscape with a distant view can symbolize expansiveness and broader horizons.

Hang a picture of mountains in your living room.

A landscape that features mountains can encourage you or family members to climb higher and achieve lofty goals.

Burn incense to "clear the air."

One of the easiest ways to chase away bad vibes in your environment is to burn incense. After an argument or upsetting incident, burn incense scented with sage, mint, or pine to clear the air and restore peace. It's a good idea to burn incense after a party, too, to get rid of the energy left behind by other people and restore balance in your home. You may also wish to do a daily cleansing ritual by burning incense in your living room each morning.

Hang faceted crystal balls in dark corners.

Does your living room have some shadowy corners? To symbolically brighten dim corners, hang small crystal or glass balls or prisms from the ceiling, preferably from red string (for good luck).

Repair or replace damaged furnishings.

Damaged, worn, or broken furnishings symbolize breaks, disappointments, or damaged relationships with friends or household members. In some cases, they can even lead to health problems. Repair or replace damaged items as soon as possible.

Promote comfortable feelings with wooly-textured fabrics.

Wooly or nubby-textured fabrics invoke the earth element and promote feelings of security, connectedness, and comfort in your home. To encourage a sense of stability and nurturing among family members, choose upholstery covered with thick, plushy fabrics, preferably in earth tones.

Replace burned-out lightbulbs.

Light augments chi and encourages clarity, optimism, and good feelings. To improve your social life as well as relationships among family members, be sure to replace lightbulbs as soon as they burn out. And remember that bright lights stimulate activity, while lower lighting promotes serenity.

Regularly clean ashes from the fireplace.

Ashes represent the past and things you no longer want or need in your life. Clean your fireplace or woodstove often to avoid these unwanted associations as well as possible safety hazards.

Use an area rug to create a sense of togetherness.

One way to strengthen symbolically the bonds among the members of your household is to place a large area rug in your living room. Make sure all the seating pieces in the room touch or rest on the rug. The rug serves as a unifying element, tying all the individual furnishings together. This decorating technique also enhances connections with friends and neighbors, and can improve your social life in general.

Include pink in your decorating scheme to encourage sociable feelings.

Pink is the color of love and sociability, so it's an ideal color to use in the living room or any area of your home where family members and guests come together. Fuchsia and magenta add a note of wisdom and spirituality; reddish pink increases passion and enthusiasm.

Freshen up your dining room with clean cloth tablecloths.

Scour linen sales and eBay for a collection of cloth tablecloths that match your decor, and keep a stack of them freshly laundered. That way, you can toss one over a sticky table or dog-hair-covered couch at a moment's notice, for example, or use it to disguise a big pile of junk that you simply don't have time to get rid of before people arrive.

Position the table so the breadwinner's chair faces the dining room's entrance.

This helps improve the breadwinner's financial prospects. Seat this person so that she or he can clearly see the entrance to the dining room. In China, it's a sign of respect to give this seat to an honored guest.

Place a round or oval rug under your table.

A round or oval rug encourages cooperation, unity, and a sense of togetherness. Place one under your dining table to promote harmonious feelings among household members. Combine an oval or round rug with a rectangular or square table to attract the benefits of both.

Don't paint your dining room white or gray.

According to the Chinese principles of feng shui, white and gray correspond to the metal element and can produce stubbornness or rigidity among household members. White is also the color of mourning in China—not a positive symbolism for dining.

Include red in your dining room's color scheme.

This lucky color should be included some place in your dining room—even if it's only a vase of red flowers on the table. Some people may find red too stimulating to use in large doses, but red walls in a dining room can give a sense of elegance in some decorating schemes.

Eat with chopsticks.

Wooden chopsticks encourage growth (as do all wooden objects). Eating with chopsticks also taps the symbolism of the number two, which can have a positive influence on partnerships.

Ring a bell or gong before dinner.

The custom of ringing a gong or bell is more than just a way to call household members to dinner. This pleasing sound breaks up stuck energy and clears the air of unwanted vibrations that might interfere with healthy digestion.

Put a live plant in your dining room.

Because the dining room has connections with money, you can improve your finances by placing a healthy, live plant in this room. Each time you water or trim the plant, you reinforce your intention to attract prosperity.

Create elemental balance on your dining table.

To establish harmony and balance, combine all five Chinese elements on your dining table. Here's an example: Set the table with ceramic dishes (earth), chopsticks (wood), crystal or glassware (water), and candles (fire) in brass holders (metal).

Bake cookies for a homey smell.

Keep a package of break-and-bake chocolate chip cookie dough on hand. You can slide a batch into the oven with just a few minutes' notice, and most guests would rather smell baking chocolate and then nosh on warm cookies than worry about whether you have a ring in the tub or a half inch of dust on the television.

Keep kitchen cabinets, drawers, and closets neat and orderly.

Closets symbolize the secret or unseen parts of our lives. In the kitchen, cabinets and closets represent the hidden factors that can influence your health and wealth. Keep these storage areas neat and orderly to avoid complications, blockages, or confusion regarding your physical or financial well-being. Go through cabinets and closets regularly, getting rid of food whose shelf life has expired or objects you no longer use.

Put round knobs on kitchen cabinets.

Kitchens tend to have lots of straight lines and sharp angles in them, which can provoke stress. Offset this by putting round knobs on cabinet doors and drawers.

Use a round kitchen table to encourage family harmony.

The circle is a universal symbol of unity. To promote harmony and cooperation among family members, put a round table in your kitchen and eat there together often.

Choose ceramic tile for beauty and durability.

Ceramic tile is easy to care for, lasts a lifetime, and enhances the appeal of any kitchen. Whether you choose Mexican-style terra-cotta for a rustic look, tiny squares for an Art Deco feel, or marble-like patterns for a sophisticated ambiance, the wide range of colors and designs offers something for everyone.

Consider installing radiant heat under the kitchen floor.

Radiant heat is the ideal solution for a kitchen. It warms up cold tiles or vinyl, and because it doesn't require baseboards or air vents, you'll have more space and flexibility when it comes to configuring cabinetry.

Choose wood floors for casual elegance.

Early American homes usually featured wooden floors in their kitchens. Oak, fir, and hard pine are traditional woods used in old kitchens, but any hardwood could be a good choice. Seal the wood with a matte polyurethane finish to waterproof it, and a wood floor becomes a practical option as well as a beautiful one. Hint: Natural wood floors look best when paired with painted cabinets. Otherwise, you can get too much of a good thing.

Use a square kitchen table to increase stability.

Squares symbolize stability and permanence. To encourage a sense of security and structure in your family, use a square table in your kitchen.

Install overhead fixtures for general illumination.

Ambient light gives overall illumination for an entire space—ceiling fixtures are the most common source of ambient light.

Choose plastic laminate countertops for economic practicality.

Plastic laminate (from Formica, Wilsonart, and other manufacturers) is the least expensive countertop option. This low-maintenance material comes in hundreds of colors, patterns, and finishes to suit virtually any décor. Add a wood edge that coordinates with your cabinets to enhance attractiveness and durability.

Leave open counter space on either side of the stove.

Allowing at least 18" (45 cm) of countertop space on either side of the stove serves two purposes. You'll have room to set food, dishes, pots, etc. while you cook. You'll also provide a safety zone—leaving one side of a stove exposed increases the chance of accidental burns, especially if there are young children in the home.

Update cabinet fixtures.

Replace old metal hardware with glass or porcelain knobs. This quick, inexpensive update transforms your kitchen immediately.

Use a glass-topped table to facilitate communication.

In the Chinese elemental system, glass belongs to the water category, whose qualities include flexibility and receptivity. To encourage easy, open communication among family members, use a kitchen table with a glass top.

Combine all five Chinese elements in your kitchen.

Feng shui is all about balance, and one way to achieve balance in your kitchen is to combine all five of the Chinese elements: earth, water, wood, fire, and metal. Most kitchens feature wooden cabinets, metal appliances, and plumbing (water). The stove represents the fire element, but earth may be lacking unless you include something made of ceramic or stone.

If possible, opt for a tile floor and/or granite countertops. If that's not an option, use pottery or stone accessories to incorporate the earth element into your kitchen.

Save nice shopping bags.

Sending leftovers or presents home with a guest? Pull out a nice shopping bag to tuck their food or gifts into, and you'll look like Martha Stewart.

Keep your towels warm.

Consider installing a drawer-style warming oven in your bathroom closet or vanity to keep towels, bathrobes, and pajamas luxuriously warm. Hint: Choose a custom drawer front to match your cabinetry.

Hang pictures in your bathroom that depict good health.

Because the bathroom is connected with health, hang images here that suggest good health and well-being.

Choose a pedestal sink for a small powder room.

Because pedestal sinks aren't as bulky as cabinet-style vanities, they're perfect for small baths and powder rooms.

Add lavender essential oil to bath water to enhance relaxation.

Lavender essential oil soothes the mind and nerves, and has a calming effect on the entire body—especially when added to bathwater. Take a hot, soothing, lavender-scented bath before bed to wash away the stress of the day and improve your sleep.

Use aromatherapy soap.

Clean-smelling mint and citrus fragrances stimulate the senses and encourage mental clarity—they're good to use first thing in the morning. Floral scents such as rose, lilac, lily of the valley, jasmine, and ylang-ylang promote affectionate feelings and congeniality. Spicy aromas—cinnamon, clove, carnation, ginger, and amber—are energizing and invigorating.

Burn candles while bathing.

Taking a bath by candlelight is both relaxing and romantic.

Install a ceiling fan in your bathroom.

This tip has both a practical and a symbolic side. A ceiling fan helps draw dampness out of the bathroom to prevent mold and mildew. A fan also circulates energy and keeps it from seeping away down the drains.

Regularly clean out your medicine cabinet.

Medications whose shelf life has lapsed can be less effective than new ones. Periodically go through your medicine cabinet and throw out old prescriptions and over-the-counter medications.

Eliminate clutter in your bathroom.

Because the bathroom is linked with health, your physical well-being may be hampered if you allow clutter to collect in this room. Keep your bathroom clean and clear to promote good health.

Add texture to your bathroom.

Smooth surfaces—tile, porcelain, glass, stainless steel—
predominate in most bathrooms. To create balance, add richly
textured materials wherever possible; try plush towels and
bath mats, a cloth shower curtain instead of glass doors, thick
curtains, or textured wallpaper. Accessories made from rough,
nubby, or nappy materials are good choices, too, instead of
the usual smooth plastic or ceramic items.

Include wood in your bathroom décor.

The wood element is missing in many bathrooms. If your bath doesn't feature a wooden vanity cabinet, add accessories made of wood, such as a wooden toilet seat, pegboard, or towel bar, or a mirror or pictures with wooden frames, to create balance. Baskets can also bring texture and the wood element into your bathroom, offsetting a predominance of the water element. They're also great for storing and organizing everything from extra rolls of toilet paper to cosmetics to guest towels.

Use large, bold patterns in your bathroom.

Large designs—especially those that feature triangles or straight lines—activate yang energy. Use bold patterns on towels, shower curtains, or wallpaper to balance a bathroom's predominant yin energy.

Make a basket o' towels for overnight guests.

This is more about money than time, but it's worth every penny if you have family members or wayfaring friends who are prone to drop by for a few nights with little or no notice. Buy and wash a couple of extra bath towels, hand towels, and washcloths; roll them up; and hide them away in a basket (even a laundry basket), along with a roll of toilet paper, a pair of clean pillowcases, and a nice new bar of soap. Next time someone shows up, you won't have to spend the night surreptitiously doing laundry before they can wash up and get to bed.

Paint bedroom walls white to strengthen commitment.

White, a "metal" color, is linked with permanence and structure. To strengthen the commitment and stability in a romantic relationship, paint the walls in your master bedroom white. Does your child have trouble focusing or completing tasks? Paint the walls in her bedroom white to improve concentration and persistence.

Use blue in your decorating scheme to promote tranquility.

Blue's soothing qualities promote feelings of tranquility and help you relax. Paint your bedroom walls blue to let you unwind at the end of the day and sleep better. Or use blue linens on your bed.

Add a clothing rod.

Many closets feature a single clothing rod that runs the entire width of a closet. Consider supplementing it with another full-length rod positioned higher for longer garments or lower for shirt and skirts. A lumber yard will cut a wooden rod to size for you—all you need to do is support it on brackets that fasten easily into place.

Avoid using a lot of red or orange in a child's room.

Red and orange are stimulating colors and may be too stressful to use in children's bedrooms. Vibrant, fiery colors can interfere with a child's sleep or concentration. In large doses, they may also promote assertiveness or tension that can lead to problems with siblings or friends. Because red is considered lucky, however, it's a good accent color.

Make use of modular storage units.

Baskets, pull-out trays, shoe racks, drawers, and other modular storage elements all expand the usable space in your closet and keep clothing neat. Incorporate them into your closet plan to maximize storage potential.

Consider building a cedar closet.

An ordinary closet can be transformed into a cedar closet
with a kit that includes interlocking pieces of aromatic cedar.
If you're selling your home, this simple update makes a good
impression on prospective buyers. Hint: For added moth
protection, hang your wool garments on cedar hangers.

In children's closets, hang clothing rods at kid height.

Make it easy for kids to hang up their clothes by installing closet rods at a height they can reach easily. Instead of a single rod that runs the width of the closet, install two rods, one above the other, to maximize storage space. Hang off-season or rarely worn clothes on the top rod and place frequently worn garments on the lower rod.

Use green in the color scheme to encourage serenity.

Green has a calming, stabilizing effect on us. Because we associate green with nature and plants, it can also help us feel secure and grounded. To help a nervous, anxious, or very active child feel more calm and centered, paint her bedroom walls green.

Hang a pleasing image on the ceiling above your bed.

Make sure the first thing you see each morning is something happy. To start your day off on the right foot, hang an attractive picture or other positive symbol on the ceiling above your bed.

Paint office walls yellow to inspire creativity.

Yellow reminds us of the sun's light and promotes feelings of warmth, optimism, and enthusiasm. It's also a good color for artists and other creative people. To encourage your own imagination, paint your office walls yellow.

Hang four pictures in your home office.

Four is the number of stability and security. To help stabilize your finances and keep money from going out faster than it comes in, hang a grouping of four pictures in your office. Make sure the images in the pictures symbolize prosperity or abundance.

Clean office windows to promote good health.

In feng shui, windows symbolize the eyes. Dirty windows cloud your ability to see clearly and may cause confusion about health matters. Washing your office windows can help you see your way to better health and well-being.

Use metal picture frames to strengthen or stabilize an area of your life.

If your goal is to strengthen family or social relationships or to promote stability in your home life, choose metal frames for artwork. Make sure the images in the pictures describe your intentions.

Position your desk so you can see the door.

Arrange your office furniture so that when you are seated at your desk you can easily see the entrance door. If your back is to the door, you may not be able to concentrate—you'll always be on guard because subconsciously you know that someone could enter your office without your knowledge. If you can't position your desk so that you can see the entrance to your office while seated, hang a mirror on the wall so that it reflects the doorway. This cure lets you glance in the mirror without having to turn around, and helps avoid distractions.

Regularly clean out your file cabinets.

If you let "old business" fill up your file cabinets, you may prevent new business from coming your way. Go through your files and update them regularly. Remove paperwork that's no longer current. A good rule of thumb is to leave about one-third of your file cabinets empty to indicate you are ready to receive new business.

Hang a pendant fixture over your keyboard.

Position a small halogen pendant fixture above your keyboard so it provides good task lighting without throwing unwanted glare onto your computer screen.

Don't place the computer in front of the window.

If you position the computer in front of the window, background sunlight will compete with the computer's screen. If you place the computer so that sunlight shines directly on the monitor, you'll run into problems, too. As you configure your home office, plan a spot for the computer that's away from the window.

Choose calming colors for your office.

Cool, soothing colors such as green, blue, gray, or tan are usually best for office environments, because they help reduce stress. However, if you work in a creative field, yellow or peach might be better choices because they stimulate imagination.

Hang a picture of a landscape in your office.

Relieve that boxed-in feeling. Hang a painting of a landscape with a distant view in your office. Periodically gaze at the picture to rest your eyes, relax your mind, and visually expand your horizons.

Keep your desktop free of clutter.

Your desktop should be considered "prime real estate," and only items you use daily should be allocated space on this work surface. A cluttered desktop is not only inefficient and unattractive, it can also signify that you are too busy to handle your current business, let alone take on anything new. Clutter is also a symbol of confusion and lack of focus. By cleaning and organizing your desk, you demonstrate a willingness to get your financial and business life in order.

Update your Rolodex regularly.

Cull old names and addresses from your Rolodex on a regular basis. You won't waste time looking through the cards of people you'll never contact again, and you'll symbolically make room for new people to enter your life.

Fix or replace damaged office equipment.

Broken or damaged equipment in your office symbolizes
broken deals or promises, damaged relationships with
customers or suppliers, and other problems. Promptly repair
or replace any office machines, computers, or furnishings to
keep your business running smoothly.

Use wooden furniture to encourage expansion.

In the Chinese elemental system, wood is linked with growth. To help your business or finances increase, furnish your office with wooden furniture.

Index